Penguin Chick

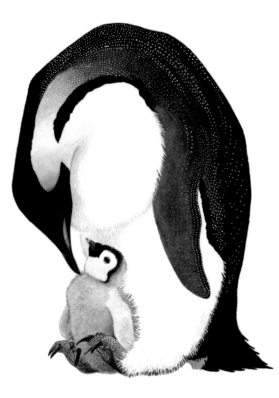

by Betty Tatham • illustrated by Helen K. Davie

HarperCollins*Publishers*

To Wendy Pfeffer, my teacher, mentor, and friend
—B.T.

To my husband, Frank, whose love and support make everything possible.
I also wish to thank Beth Dirksen, senior aviculturist at Sea World San Diego.
I am grateful for her enthusiasm and invaluable advice, and for arranging my
unforgettable (but chilly) visit "up close" with the emperors.
—H.K.D.

Special thanks to marine biologist Frank S. Todd, executive director of
EcoCepts International, who has studied and observed emperor penguins in
Antarctica for more than twenty-five years.

The *Let's-Read-and-Find-Out Science* book series was originated by Dr. Franklyn M. Branley, Astronomer Emeritus and former Chairman of the American Museum–Hayden Planetarium, and was formerly co-edited by him and Dr. Roma Gans, Professor Emeritus of Childhood Education, Teachers College, Columbia University. Text and illustrations for each of the books in the series are checked for accuracy by an expert in the relevant field. For more information about Let's-Read-and-Find-Out Science books, write to HarperCollins Children's Books, 195 Broadway, New York, NY 10007, or visit our website at www.letsreadandfindout.com.

Penguin Chick
Text copyright © 2002 by Betty Tatham
Illustrations copyright © 2002 by Helen K. Davie
Manufactured in China. All rights reserved.

Library of Congress Cataloging-in-Publication Data
Tatham, Betty.
  Penguin chick / by Betty Tatham ; illustrated by Helen K. Davie.
    p.   cm.—(Let's-read-and-find-out science. Stage 2)
  ISBN 0-06-028594-X — ISBN 0-06-028595-8 (lib. bdg.) — ISBN 0-06-445206-9 (pbk.)
  1. Emperor penguin—Infancy—Juvenile literature. [1. Emperor penguin. 2. Penguins.
3. Parental behavior in animals.] I. Davie, Helen, ill. II. Title. III. Series.
QL696.S473 T37 2002
598.47—dc21   00-059696

Typography by Elynn Cohen   15 16 17 SCP 20 19 18 17 16   ❖   First Edition

Penguin Chick

A fierce wind howls. It whips snow across the ice.

Here, a female emperor penguin has just laid an egg. It is the only egg she will lay this year.

Most birds build nests for their eggs. But on the ice in Antarctica, there are no twigs or leaves. There is no grass or mud. Nothing to build a nest with. Nothing but snow and ice.

5

The new penguin father uses his beak to scoop the egg onto his webbed feet.

He tucks it under his feather-covered skin, into a special place
called a brood patch. The egg will be as snug and warm there as
if it were in a sleeping bag.

One of the penguin parents must stay with the egg to keep it warm. But where penguins lay their eggs, there is no food for them to eat.

The penguin father is bigger and fatter than the mother. He can live longer without food. So the father penguin stays with the egg while the mother travels to the sea to find food.

The two parents sing together before the mother penguin leaves.

Along with many other penguins, the mother penguin leaves the rookery, where she laid her egg.

The mother walks or slides on her belly. This is called
tobogganing. She uses her flippers and webbed feet to
push herself forward over ice and snow.

Because it's winter in Antarctica, water near the shore is frozen for many miles. After three days the mother penguin comes to the end of the ice. She dives into the water to hunt for fish, squid, and tiny shrimplike creatures called krill.

FISH

SQUID

KRILL

Back at the rookery, the penguin
fathers form a group called a huddle.
They stand close together for warmth.
Each one keeps his own egg warm.

14

For two months the penguin father always keeps his egg on his feet. When he walks, he shuffles his feet so the egg doesn't roll away. He sleeps standing up. He has no food to eat, but the fat on his body keeps him alive.

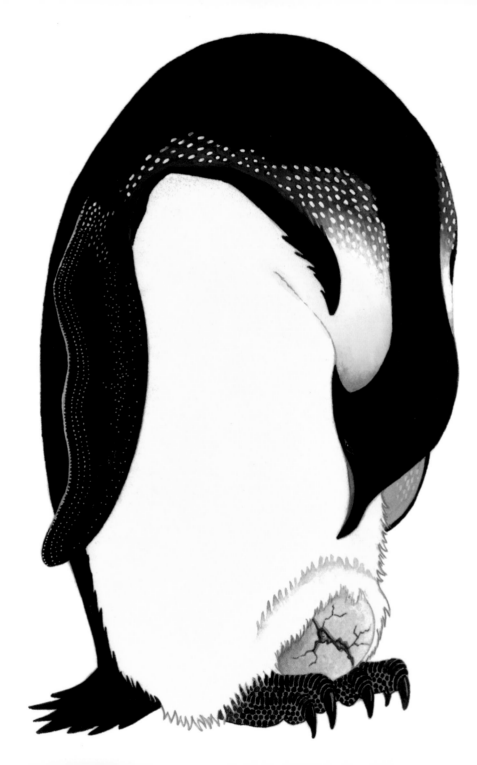

Finally he feels the chick move inside the egg. The chick pecks and pecks and pecks. In about three days the egg cracks open.

The chick is wet. But soon his soft feathers, called down, dry and become fluffy and gray. The father still keeps the chick warm in the brood patch. Sometimes the chick pokes his head out. But while he's so little, he must stay covered. And he must stay on his father's feet. Otherwise the cold would kill him.

The father talks to the chick in his trumpet voice. The chick answers with a whistle.

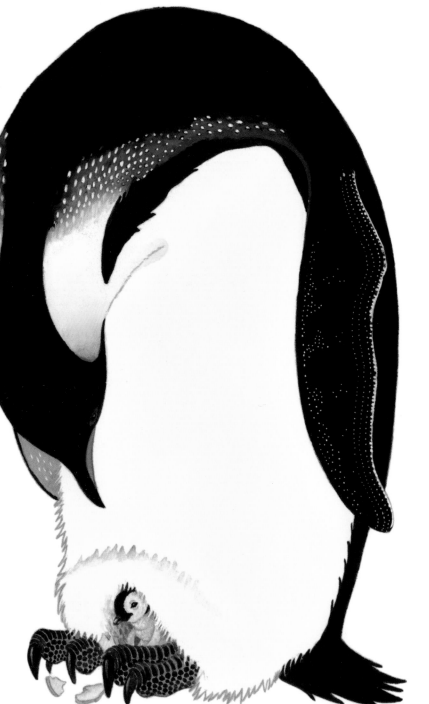

The father's trumpet call echoes across the ice. The penguin mother is on her way back to the rookery, but she can't hear him. She's still too far away. If the mother doesn't come back soon with food, the chick will die.

Two days pass before the mother can hear the father penguin's call.

At last the mother arrives at the rookery. She cuddles close
to her chick and trumpets to him. He whistles back. With
her beak she brushes his soft gray down.

The mother swallowed many fish before she left the ocean. She brings some of this food back up from her stomach and feeds her chick. She has enough food to keep him fed for weeks. He stays on her feet and snuggles into her brood patch.

The father is very hungry, so he travels to open water. There he dives to hunt for food. Weeks later the father returns with more food for the chick.

Each day the parents preen, or brush, the chick's downy coat with their beaks. This keeps the down fluffy and keeps the chick warm.

As the chick gets bigger, he and the other chicks no longer need to stay on their parents' feet. Instead they stay together to keep warm.

This group of chicks is called a crèche, or a nursery. The chick now spends most of his time here. But he still rushes to his mother or father to be fed when either one comes back from the ocean.

Sometimes the chick and the other young penguins dig their beaks into the ice to help them walk up a slippery hill. They toboggan down fast on their fluffy bellies.

The chick grows and grows. After five months, he has grown into a junior penguin. He is old enough to travel to the ocean.

WINTER		SPRING	
AUGUST	SEPTEMBER	OCTOBER

Now he has a waterproof coat of feathers, instead of fluffy down. He can swim in the icy cold ocean because his feathers keep him dry and warm.

		SUMMER
NOVEMBER	DECEMBER	JANUARY

The young penguin spends most of his time in the water. He swims, flapping his flippers as if he were flying underwater. He uses his webbed feet to steer wherever he wants to go.

He catches a fish with his beak and swallows it headfirst.

Now the young penguin can catch his own food and take care of himself. In about five years he'll find a mate. Then he'll take care of his own egg until the chick can hatch.

FIND OUT MORE ABOUT PENGUINS

There are seventeen different kinds of penguins. All penguins catch their food in the ocean. They live on fish, squid, or shrimplike krill. Only emperor penguins lay their eggs on ice. All other penguins lay their eggs on land, and most build nests.

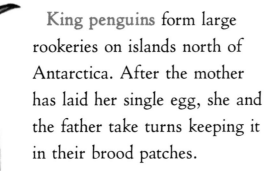

King penguins form large rookeries on islands north of Antarctica. After the mother has laid her single egg, she and the father take turns keeping it in their brood patches.

Sometimes hundreds of Adélie penguins live in one rookery on the coast of Antarctica. In the spring Adélies build nests of stones and pebbles. Parents lie on the nest and tuck the eggs into their brood patches. They take two-week turns.

Adélie

King

Rockhopper

Rockhoppers often jump into the ocean feetfirst, instead of diving in like many other penguins. They build stone nests in large rookeries on islands. The mother lays two eggs but can raise only one chick. The stronger of the two chicks survives.

Jackass penguins bray like jackasses or donkeys. They live on the southern coast of Africa. With their beaks and feet, jackasses dig nesting tunnels in the soil. If the soil is too hard to dig, they build nests of roots, twigs, and sometimes pebbles on top of the ground.

Little blues, or fairy penguins, are the smallest penguins. They live in Australia and New Zealand. Little blues make their nests out of dirt and stones in burrows and caves. The mother lays two eggs, and the parents take turns keeping the eggs warm and feeding the two chicks.

Jackass

Little blue

Walk Like a Penguin

Take off your shoes and hold your feet close together. Put a raw potato on your feet. Walk by shuffling your feet forward just a little at a time. This is how penguin fathers walk when they're carrying their eggs. Be careful not to drop your "egg"!

Toboggan Like a Penguin

Lie down on a smooth surface such as a bare floor. Use your hands and arms to push yourself forward. Your toes can help too. This is how penguins toboggan over ice and snow.